GOATs IN SPORTS

SOCCER GOATs

KENNY ABDO

Fly!
An Imprint of Abdo Zoom
abdobooks.com

abdobooks.com

Published by Abdo Zoom, a division of ABDO, P.O. Box 398166, Minneapolis, Minnesota 55439. Copyright © 2025 by Abdo Consulting Group, Inc. International copyrights reserved in all countries. No part of this book may be reproduced in any form without written permission from the publisher. Fly!™ is a trademark and logo of Abdo Zoom.

Printed in the United States of America, North Mankato, Minnesota.
052024
092024

Photo Credits: Getty Images, Shutterstock
Production Contributors: Kenny Abdo, Jennie Forsberg, Grace Hansen
Design Contributors: Candice Keimig, Neil Klinepier

Library of Congress Control Number: 2023948519

Publisher's Cataloging-in-Publication Data

Names: Abdo, Kenny, author.
Title: Soccer GOATs / by Kenny Abdo.
Description: Minneapolis, Minnesota : Abdo Zoom, 2025 | Series: GOATs in sports | Includes online resources and index.
Identifiers: ISBN 9781098285678 (lib. bdg.) | ISBN 9781098286378 (ebook) | ISBN 9781098286729 (Read-to-me eBook)
Subjects: LCSH: Soccer--Juvenile literature. | European football--Juvenile literature. | Soccer--Records--Juvenile literature. | World Cup (Soccer)--Juvenile literature. | Professional athletes--Juvenile literature.
Classification: DDC 796.334--dc23

TABLE OF CONTENTS

Soccer GOATs 4

The Greats 8

Scoreboard 20

Glossary 22

Online Resources 23

Index 24

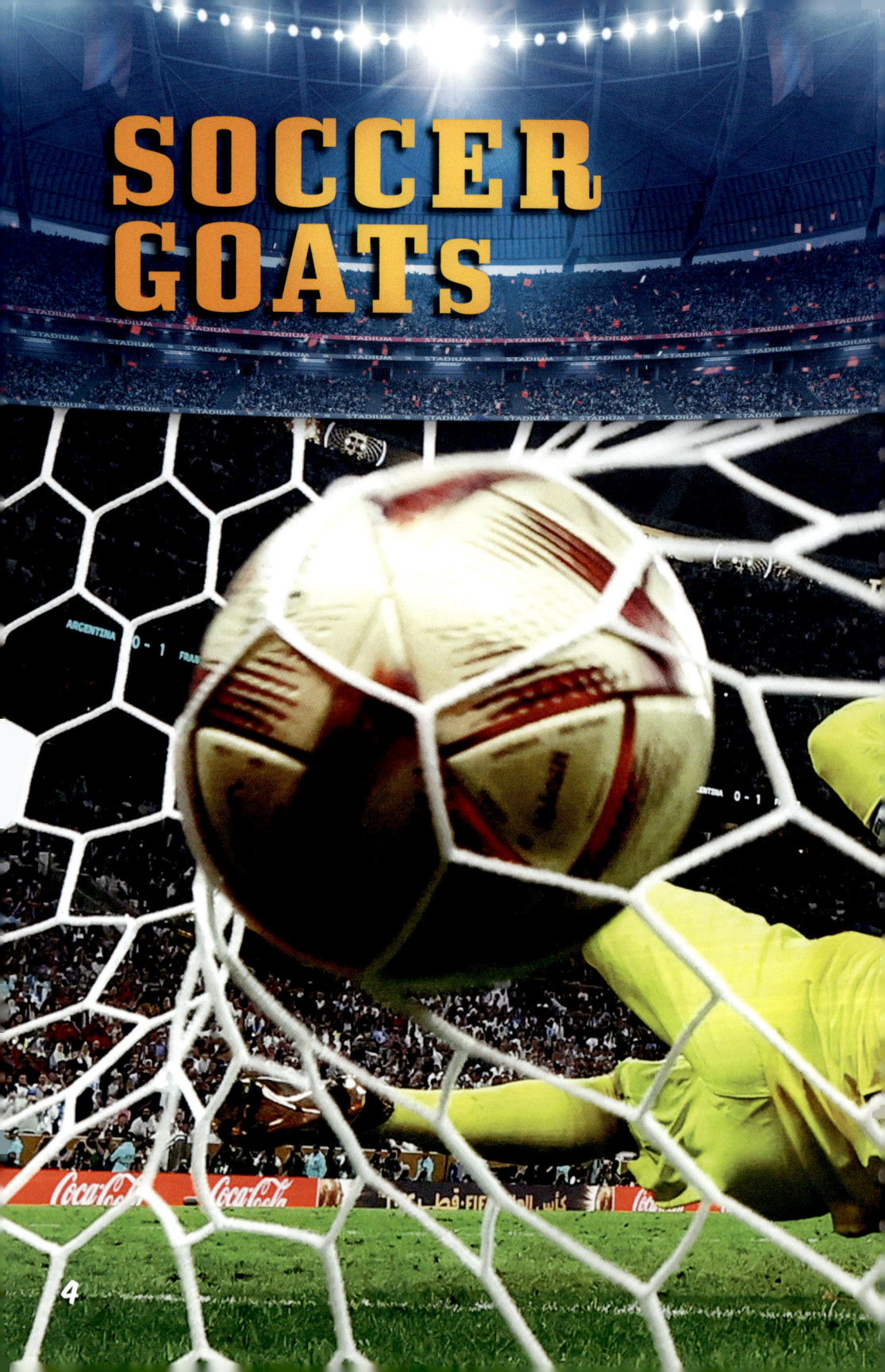
SOCCER GOATs

As the most-watched sport in the world, all eyes are on the GOATs of soccer!

From Pelé to Lionel Messi, the greatest soccer players have dribbled their way into history!

THE GREATS

At the age of 17, Pelé became the youngest player to win a **World Cup**. After two more World Cup wins, he left Brazil in 1975 to play in the United States. Pelé retired in 1977 with more than 1,000 goals and widely regarded as one of the greatest players of all time!

Johan Cruyff played many positions for many teams during his career. He won three European Cups in a row. With three goals and three assists, Cruyff helped lead the Netherlands to the final of the 1974 **World Cup**. He snatched a **Golden Ball** for the tournament. He also created a popular move, the Cruyff Turn.

Franz Beckenbauer is one of nine players to have won the **World Cup**, the European Champions Cup, and the **Golden Ball**! He won a total of 18 major trophies as a player.

Diego Maradona won many awards with many teams. He snagged two **Serie A** titles with Napoli. Maradona received the **Golden Ball** award after winning the 1986 **World Cup**! He is considered one of the best, behind only Pelé and Messi.

As a midfielder, Michel Platini scored like a forward. He hit a record nine goals during the 1984 European Championship. Platini retired in 1987 after France reached the semi-finals at the 1986 **World Cup**. His 41 international goals were the most for any French player at the time.

Mia Hamm started on the United States women's national soccer team at just 15 years old. She won the Women's **World Cup** in 1991 and 1999. Hamm also claimed two **Olympic** gold medals. She was voted into the National Soccer **Hall of Fame** in 2007.

Zinedine Zidane played on many European teams and the France national team, winning the **World Cup**, the **Champions League**, and the **Golden Ball**! He became the first French coach for Real Madrid in 2016!

Ronaldo's incredible skills and scoring earned him the nickname "Il Fenomeno." He was the first player to win **FIFA's** Player of the Year award two years in a row. Ronaldo played 98 matches with Brazil and scored 62 goals, making him the third-highest goalscorer for his national team.

Marta is a player so powerful, she's known by just one name. She helped make Brazil a powerful team too. Marta has led Brazil to both the **World Cup** and the **Olympics**. In 2006, she won her first of five consecutive World Player of the Year Awards, adding a sixth in 2018.

Lionel Messi played his first professional match for Barcelona at 16 years old in 2003. The next year, he made his senior **debut** and the goals started to pile up for Barcelona. He racked up nearly 700 goals in 17 years. In 2021, Messi brought international glory to Argentina when he helped his team win the **Copa América**.

Players like Marta and Messi have revealed how far they will go on the field to be the best. After all, becoming the GOAT is always a great goal to have!

GLOSSARY

Champions League – a yearly soccer competition organized by the Union of European Football Associations (UEFA).

Copa América – the top men's soccer tournament played by the national teams of South America.

FIFA – the international organization for men's and women's soccer.

Golden Ball – an award given to the FIFA World Cup tournament's best player.

Hall of Fame – the group of highly celebrated people honored for their achievements in a sport or other activity. In soccer, it is called the National Soccer Hall of Fame.

Olympic – of or relating to the Olympic Games. The Games are the biggest international athletic events held as separate winter and summer competitions.

Serie A – the highest division of professional soccer in Italy and one of the Big Five leagues in all of Europe.

World Cup – an international soccer competition held every four years.

ONLINE RESOURCES

To learn more about the GOATs in Soccer, please visit **abdobooklinks.com** or scan this QR code. These links are routinely monitored and updated to provide the most current information available.

INDEX

Argentina 18

Barcelona 18

Beckenbauer, Franz 11

Brazil 8, 16, 17

Cruyff, Johan 10

France 13, 15

Hamm, Mia 14

Maradona, Diego 12

Marta 17, 21

Messi, Lionel 7, 12, 18, 21

Napoli 12

North America 8

Olympics 14, 17

Pelé 7, 8, 12

Platini, Michel 13

Ronaldo 16

Zidane, Zinedine 15